TRUTH
IN OUR
TIME

DR. PAUL KELM

Published by Straight Talk Books
P.O. Box 301, Milwaukee, WI 53201
800.661.3311 · timeofgrace.org

Copyright © 2021 Time of Grace Ministry

All rights reserved. This publication may not be copied, photocopied, reproduced, translated, or converted to any electronic or machine-readable form in whole or in part, except for brief quotations, without prior written approval from Time of Grace Ministry.

Unless otherwise indicated, Scripture is taken from THE HOLY BIBLE, NEW INTERNATIONAL VERSION®, NIV®. Copyright © 1973, 1978, 1984, 2011 by Biblica, Inc.® Used by permission. All rights reserved worldwide.

Scripture marked ESV is taken from The Holy Bible, English Standard Version. Copyright © 2001 by Crossway Bibles, a publishing ministry of Good News Publishers.

Scripture marked NKJV is taken from the New King James Version®. Copyright © 1982 by Thomas Nelson. Used by permission. All rights reserved.

Printed in the United States of America

ISBN: 978-1-949488-54-8

TIME OF GRACE *is a registered mark of Time of Grace Ministry.*

Contents

What's This About? 5

Truth in Our Time.. 6

Whatever Happened to Truth? 8

Truth or Consequences 13

There *Is* a Conspiracy 17

The God's Honest Truth 24

The Truth Hurts 30

The Truth Will Set You Free 34

Half-Truths and Big Lies..39

    "That may be your truth, but it's not my truth." 39

    "We all have a bit of the truth. No one has the whole truth." ... 42

    "It's not a lie if you believe it to be true." 47

    "It's my body. I can do what I want with it." 51

    "The heart wants what the heart wants."...................... 56

    "You owe it to yourself to do what makes you happy." 60

    "You have to learn to love yourself." 65

    "If you can think it, you can do it."............................. 69

    "It's okay as long as nobody gets hurt." 73

    "It's just sex."... 77

    "Don't be so intolerant." 81

    "YOLO" 85

To Tell the Truth..89

What's This About?

A meme going around has a portrait of George Washington and the caption, "Can't tell a lie." It's followed by a picture of a recent president and the caption, "Can't tell the truth." Finally, there's a picture of a more recent president and the caption, "Can't tell the difference." It is meant to be funny. It isn't. Has our culture lost respect for the truth? Can we even define truth? And do you expect to hear the truth? The first half of this book will explore the state of truth telling in America and how we got to this point, as well as remind you that there is still absolute truth from God in his Word. The second half of the book will dissect 12 popular statements that mask serious lies with *truthy*-sounding platitudes. At the close of the book, you will be encouraged to do your part to restore truth in our time—as St. Paul put it, **"speaking the truth in love"** (Ephesians 4:15).

Truth in Our Time

The title *Truth in Our Time* conveys sad irony, for truth in our time is not what people two or more generations ago understood it to be. Truth for centuries meant absolute fact, objective reality. Truth conveyed moral certainty. Truth was a brilliant clarity in contrast with the darkness of a lie or the murky gray of deception. You could state a truth with confidence that others understood your words precisely. Witnesses in court swore to tell the truth, the whole truth, and nothing but the truth. Today truth is blurred with opinion so that different people can have their own version of the truth. Truth

There is . . . absolute, objective, universal truth.

is twisted into propaganda, with facts chosen selectively to support a moral argument or a political position. We're told that truth depends on one's culture and experience, as though geography, race, socioeconomic conditions, and upbringing shape a person's truth; and your truth may therefore be different from my truth. It's confusing. How do you know what to believe?

Still, there is truth in our time—absolute, objective, universal truth. An unchanging God has spoken truth in Scripture, hard facts about humanity and life as well as divine assurances about God and our place with him. The reality of who we are, how we got here, what life is worth, and what happens when life ends doesn't change with cultural perspectives or individual feelings. Right and wrong have a clear basis, apart from the decisions of legislatures, courts, and opinion shapers. Amid the fog of intellectual arguments, media-driven hype, and personal opinion, truth from God stands the test of time and provides a litmus test for whatever you read or hear, an answer for the things that make you wonder whether you should accept them.

Let's begin with a brief overview of how we got to this point of truth confusion.

Whatever Happened to Truth?

The assault on truth has a history. You might not be interested in the philosophical twists and turns of the plot, words like *existentialism, nihilism,* and *postmodernism.* But those intellectual schools of thought have been popularized by movies, television series, advertising, and social media. There are slogans repeated by celebrities and protesters. There are college courses and best sellers that translate philosophy into lifestyles. Carried along by a cultural tide, we may not notice the many elements of our culture that have chipped away at truth. Here are a few.

For well over a century, so-called scholars have questioned the Bible. They made assumptions about the authorship of biblical books, challenging the previously held conviction that God inspired Scripture through human writers. They rejected miracles as sacred myth accepted by unenlightened people. What was called "the search for the historical Jesus" ignored actual history in favor of pointy-headed opinions about who Jesus was and what he said. In too many mainline religious denominations, this undercutting of God's Word became the fare of sermons and books. Little by little biblical truth was eroded until people were left with a faith lacking real content.

The term *pluralism* moved from acknowledging that there are many different religions and cultures to suggesting that these various religions and cultures are equally valid. It would be intolerant, we've been told, to claim that one way of viewing and practicing life is superior to others. Therefore, a Hindu's "truth" is as good as a Muslim's "truth" or a Christian's truth. People who practice a polygamous family life are no less moral than those who view marriage as one man and one woman. And who are you to tell anyone else how to live, right? A corollary to philosophical pluralism is the idea that there is no one overarching story such as the Bible's that explains life. Different people simply have different stories, and the stories don't have to come together to make sense of life. Life is rather a random series of events. The Bible's creation-to-kingdom-come explanation for life is rejected in favor of the notion that life has no meaning; it just is.

Pragmatism is the claim that the only real truth guide is "what works." If a group of people find satisfaction and meaning in a lifestyle that was once considered morally wrong, if it works for them, then it is their truth. If abortion solves the problem of unwanted pregnancies, then that is what works. When enough people agree, laws change with changing opinion. On an individual basis, pragmatism has been reduced to the mantra: "It works for me." The question of what is true becomes irrelevant. What makes me happy is what must be true for me.

What makes me happy is what must be true for me.

Reason and logic gave way to emotion and intuition. And since emotion and intuition are personal and subjective, there is no basis for positing truth that is true for everyone everywhere. Our conversation demonstrates the shift from reason-based to emotion-driven approaches to life. Fifty years ago, a person might ask a friend, "What do you *think* about nuclear power plants?" Today that question will likely be, "How do you *feel* about nuclear power plants?"

History, in today's intellectual climate, has been moved from the realm of fact to the category of propaganda—the story told by whoever is dominant, whoever won the war or imposed their will. Don't worry about the facts. What you emphasize in history becomes the meaning of history—your version of the truth.

Perhaps you've noticed a shift from the word *morality* to *ethics* and then to *values*. Morality has the sound of objective right and wrong. Ethics implies consensus-built standards for an industry or a profession. Values are personal—my idea of what is right or wrong. Values can then turn what *is* into what *should be.*

Educated elites no longer believe that truth can be articulated in words. "Deconstruction" is the approach in literary circles that claims meaning can only be found in the intersection of words with individual perspectives. Words don't mean the same thing to different people because of their different life experiences, their education, their view of life. If this is true, then we can't be sure that what we mean with a sentence is what someone else will understand in that sentence. When I say the word *family*, some may hear father, mother, and the kids while others hear a group of people who share a place and a lifestyle. Therefore, words cannot adequately convey universal truth or meaning. If that sounds sort of fuzzy, it's because that is how truth is left—sort of fuzzy.

In the absence of real truth, cynicism reigns.

If all this has left you feeling pessimistic about not just truth but life, you're not alone. In the absence of real truth, cynicism reigns. If there is no absolute truth, no central and unifying purpose to life, no history that explains how we got here, and no hope for the future, no possibility of arriving at a sure knowledge of anything . . . if life isn't going anywhere but in circles . . . then cynical pessimism is the inevitable conclusion. Here are a few "Proverbs of Postmodernism" that appeared on the internet:

"The facts, although interesting, are irrelevant."
"I have seen the truth, and it makes no sense."
"Happiness is merely the remission of pain."
"Sometimes too much to drink is not enough."
"Suicide is the most sincere form of self-criticism."
"Anything worth fighting for is worth fighting dirty for."
"Not one shred of evidence supports the notion that life is serious."

Bleak!

Whatever happened to truth. That word *whatever* has become a way to dismiss any serious attempt to arrive at truth. Try to tell a teenager an important life lesson, and you may hear back: "Whatever." Explain why you are concerned about a friend's life choices, and the response may be, "Whatever." *Whatever* may mean "I don't care" or "It doesn't matter" or "That's just your opinion," but it shuts down conversation. *Whatever* happened to truth.

Think About It

How many truths about life that you were taught as a child have been rejected in contemporary culture?

Who are the people you are supposed to listen to in today's world? How did they earn that right?

What are some signs that pessimism about life in today's world is turning into cynicism? How can you help a friend whose view of life has moved God away from the center and turned cynical?

Truth or Consequences

When truth is distorted and denied, there are consequences. You've witnessed these consequences, and many of them have angered you. Worse, you may unwittingly have come to accept distortions of truth. And sadly, you may be intimidated into silence when you are confronted by falsehoods that are told repeatedly by influential people.

The term *spin doctor* was invented to describe someone who can articulate an upside to a politician's failures or an illegality in business. Persecution by the press is the spin that obscures the bad judgment of a senator. Research to find a cure for another disease is the positive spin for price gouging on a patented medication. It's like a magician's sleight of hand. A spin doctor can get us to look over there and not notice what is happening over here. This is bending the truth, stretching the truth, looking for a way to hide the truth. And we are fast learners. We can spin our selfish acts into attempts to be kind. We can hide our wrongs by pointing to the wrongs of others. We may even believe our spin because in contemporary culture we can create our own truth.

You may unwittingly have come to accept distortions of truth.

Marketers will tell you that "perception is reality." In other words, the facts don't matter when it comes to how people shop or vote. What matters is how they feel about things, how their peers look at things, what they can be led to believe about things. From advertising to press conferences, the goal is to shape our perception of things.

Disinformation is what a nation's enemies spread to shape opinions and influence elections. The radio voice of Tokyo Rose in World War II has given way to manipulating opinion via today's social media platforms. Russia does it. Conspiracy theorists do it. And we are left wondering what to believe.

"Fake news" is a relatively recent concept, actual lies dressed up as real facts in order to mislead people to think the way shadowy influencers have decided we should think. And real news, true facts, can be dismissed when a popular figure calls them fake news. As a result, people distrust news sources that don't align with their own political convictions. And the populace is divided into angry camps.

The populace is divided into angry camps.

Political correctness is a recent term for cultural peer pressure. "Correct" is not the same as true or morally right. How we should feel about same-sex marriage, for example, is conditioned by a lobbying group or social shaming. Silencing truth is a consequence of political correctness.

Statistical morality has replaced objective right and wrong. Polls will tell us how large a percentage of the population believes that the freedom to indulge in sex with multiple partners is morally acceptable. And if enough people do something, it becomes "natural" or "normal." Again, what *is* thereby becomes what *should be*. And woe to the person who objects on the basis of "doctrine" (which has become a dirty word).

Cancel culture is a term invented to describe efforts to reframe history and silence what doesn't fit with a vocal minority's opinion. If what happened in the past doesn't square with how people today feel about those events, simply deny or obscure the events. Historical revisionism is not new. Egyptian pharaohs and Russian dictators used their power to rewrite history. Now social movements can do it with political pressure. Facts are irrelevant.

Conspiracy theories abound when people are not held to a truth standard, when spin and fake news have made people suspicious of government, social institutions, and elected officials. We actually expect leaders to lie to us. Distrust of authority makes people susceptible to a charismatic voice or a reactionary movement. When we don't know what to believe, we gravitate toward those who prey on our fears and offer change. The net result is a very polarized population of fearful and angry people.

Comedian Stephen Colbert coined the term *truthiness* for ideas that sound sort of right and loudly proclaim agendas that resonate with our instincts. In the absence of honesty and factual reporting, with the loss of moral standards and objective truth, we are left with "truthiness"—a pale imitation of truth masking an effort to manipulate our thinking. It has come to this.

Already two millennia ago, the apostle Paul warned what would happen when truth is shunted aside: **"For the time will come when people will not put up with sound doctrine. Instead, to suit their own desires, they will gather around them a great number of teachers to say what their itching ears want to hear. They will turn their ears away from the truth and turn aside to myths"** (2 Timothy 4:3,4).

Think About It

Can you suggest examples of how parents use "spin" in talking with their children or how friends spin the facts in order to make themselves look good?

Why might you believe a conspiracy theory? Does the answer lie in the conspiracy theory, in your altered view of life, or in something else?

Whom do you trust to tell you the truth?

There *Is* a Conspiracy

It is important to identify the origin of a pandemic, an internet hack, a terrorist plot, or a shipment of illegal drugs. We can't understand or stop what we don't identify. So where do lies, deceptions, and half-truths come from? Is all this assault on truth a random, disconnected set of events, or is there a dark and shadowy conspiracy behind the redefinition and rejection of truth? No, this isn't an international cabal of oligarchs and deep state operatives. QAnon is not the source, nor is Antifa. Listen to Jesus as he addresses a hostile audience: **"You belong to your father, the devil, and you want to carry out your father's desires. He was a murderer from the beginning, not holding to the truth, for there is no truth in him. When he lies, he speaks his native language, for he is a liar and the father of lies"** (John 8:44). A spiritual pandemic—and that's what the rejection of truth is—has a spiritual source, and we'd better confront that reality.

St. Paul put it this way: **"For our struggle is not against flesh and blood, but against the rulers, against the authorities, against the powers of this dark world and against the spiritual forces of evil in the heavenly realms. Therefore put on the full armor of God, so that when the day of evil comes, you may be able to stand your ground"** (Ephesians 6:12,13). Satan prefers to remain anonymous. He and the demons who follow him would like us to scoff at the notion of evil personified. Unmasking the source of deceit is a critical first step in defeating the lies.

Can people be unwittingly deluded to believe a lie? Every cult confirms that this is true. Can a society be misled to accept wrong as right, evil as natural, falsehood as a version of truth? How else do you explain the complicity of the German populace in Adolph Hitler's *final solution*? So how did Satan convince so many that the truth of the past has been overruled by the "enlightened" ideas of the present? How could people arrive at the conclusion that killing babies in the womb is a constitutionally guaranteed right? How could intelligent people believe that, contrary to biological science, there are multiple genders and individuals can choose to be the gender they feel like or prefer? How has promiscuous sex become accepted as "natural" or that theft is justified as "reparations" if you are an oppressed minority? **Something has happened to turn reality upside down.**

We can learn something from the temptations of Satan recorded in Scripture. At the dawn of creation, Satan—a powerful angel who rejected God's will and rule—tempted Adam and Eve with this approach:

"He said to the woman, 'Did God really say, "You must not eat from any tree in the garden"?' The woman said to the serpent, 'We may eat fruit from the trees in the garden, but God did say, "You must not eat fruit from the tree that is in the middle of the garden, and you must not touch it, or you will die."' 'You will not certainly die,' the serpent said to the woman. 'For God knows that when you eat from it your eyes will be opened, and you will be like God, knowing good and evil.' When the woman saw that the fruit of the tree was good for food and pleasing to the eye, and also desirable for gaining wisdom, she took some and ate it. She also gave some to her husband, who was with her, and he ate it" (Genesis 3:1-6).

Recognize the devil's *modus operandi*: "Did God really say?" Satan leads us to question authority, challenge the source of truth. He makes us wonder if we've been misled. Doubt. And Eve expanded what God had said to make his command seem unreasonable. People still create a caricature of God's will to make God seem unreasonable, to rationalize their sinful choices.

Then Satan suggests a big lie backed by a half-truth. Death, the consequence of ignoring God's command, is simply dismissed—a huge lie. And who wouldn't want to be like God, deciding for themselves what is right and wrong, controlling their own destiny? But what Satan offered he couldn't deliver. He had himself tried to replace God and failed. Human beings would fare no better. Next comes a half-truth. Yes, Adam and Eve would know good and evil, but by choosing evil they would separate themselves from their Creator and own evil in their very nature.

Finally, there is temptation in the guise of fruit that looks good and incites desire. Lies are sold on the basis of their appeal, what looks good or sounds good. Well, can Satan's conspiracy really be that simple? Challenging the age-old wisdom of God's Word, offering what harmonizes with the desire to be in control of your own life, suggesting a claim that resonates with our sensual desires? Think about it.

Look at how Satan tempted Jesus: **"Then Jesus was led by the Spirit into the wilderness to be tempted by the devil. After fasting forty days and forty nights, he was hungry. The tempter came to him and said, 'If you are the Son of God, tell these stones to become bread.' Jesus answered, 'It is written: "Man shall not live on bread alone, but on every word that comes from the mouth of God."' Then the devil took him to the holy city and had him stand on the highest point of the temple. 'If you are the Son of God,'** he said, 'throw yourself down. For it is written: "He will command his angels concerning you, and they will lift you up in their hands, so that you will not strike your foot against a stone."' Jesus answered him, 'It is also written: "Do not put the Lord your God to the test."' Again, the devil took him to a very high mountain and showed him all the kingdoms of the world and their splendor. 'All this I will give you,' he said, 'if you will bow down and worship me.' Jesus said to him, 'Away from me, Satan! For it is written: "Worship the Lord your God, and serve him only"'" (Matthew 4:1-10).

Recognize the devil's *modus operandi*. He knows that people are more susceptible to his machinations when they are vulnerable. Jesus was alone and famished when the devil came to him. When we are hurt and frustrated, we are willing to look for someone to blame; and that sets us on a path of resentment, bitterness, and anger. When we've suffered an injustice, we can too easily legitimize unhealthy feelings about what we are owed, what we deserve. Grief, loneliness, ill health, the loss of a job—these and other emotion-filled circumstances open the door to manipulation by the minions of our archenemy, the devil.

IF is a big little word. It questions our assumptions, makes us defensive, challenges our convictions. "Prove you're the Son of God," the devil demanded. We're not Jesus. When we are asked to defend what we believe or prove that God is right, we can be led onto an intellectual battlefield of doubts. Someone who is more intelligent, more articulate, and better versed on a subject can lead us to wonder if what we've always believed is still true.

IF is a big little word.

The devil and those he co-opts will even quote the Bible out of context in a kind of verbal judo. Jesus recognized the misuse of Psalm 91. We may not. You've heard a cynic say, "I thought you Christians were supposed to . . ." or, "If you really believed what you claim to believe . . ." A skillful debater can twist truth to make it seem unreliable. The argument "Yes, but . . ." dismisses truth and seeks to lead us on a path of feelings or experiences rather than rationality.

The devil's big lie to Jesus was that the world was Satan's to give, that Jesus' mission was to reclaim the world from Satan's control. In effect, the devil's argument was that there was an easier way than the path of suffering that lay ahead for the Savior. Satan shifted the focus from humankind's relationship with God, from forgiveness and salvation, to the glitter of materialism and the desire for control. Jesus saw through the deception. The so-called "deal with the devil" is still our relationship with God in exchange for material wealth or sensual satisfaction. Satan would love to have us believe that there is an easier way, a shortcut that only bends the rules. He appeals to our desire to be in control of our circumstances, to be in charge of our lives, to avoid suffering. A big lie of the past century and a half is utopianism, the notion that you can have a kind of heaven on earth where you have no fears or worries, where everyone is equally cared for and prosperous, where your desires are met. Marxist Communism, not surprisingly atheistic, is an expression of that lie. The brutal dictatorship of Joseph Stalin, Mao, Pol Pot, and others demonstrates how big a lie this is. On a much smaller scale, we are each tempted to seek or create our own little version of utopia—life the way we want it.

More important than identifying the devil's game is to appreciate the Savior's response. Each time Jesus quoted Scripture. Why? Because Scripture is truth, and the one way to answer lies and delusions and half-truths is with absolute truth, divine truth.

The conspiracy led by Satan is not new. The apostle Paul wrote in Colossians chapter 2: In Christ **"are hidden all the treasures of wisdom and knowledge. I tell you this so that no one may deceive you by fine-sounding arguments. . . . See to it that no one takes you captive through hollow and deceptive philosophy, which depends on human tradition and the elemental spiritual forces of this world rather than on Christ"** (verses 3,4,8). Fine-sounding arguments, hollow and deceptive philosophy, spiritual forces of this world. Recognize the conspiracy.

Think About It

Analyze how many deceptions and denials of truth in our time follow the same pattern established in the Garden of Eden. And appreciate the consequences.

What is the caricature of a Bible-believing Christian that Satan has created in our time?

How many lies in our time are sold on the basis of science or the credibility of PhDs and celebrities?

The God's Honest Truth

If you want to know how something works, ask the inventor. If you want to understand the meaning of an abstract painting, listen to the artist. If you want to know the truth about something that happened, let the person who was there tell you. Seems obvious, until a human-centered culture approaches the subject of truth. God is the Creator of life, so it stands to reason that we should listen to his explanation of what life is, how it is best lived, and what it is worth. But if evolution replaces creation, we have no one to ask about life truths, and it's a short road to denying the existence of absolute truth. Christianity is a historical faith: rooted in the facts of God's intervention in human history; culminating in the entrance of God's Son into history to live, die, and rise for our salvation. God was there in every significant event of salvation history. He recorded what happened in the Bible. Reject the historicity of the Bible and what is left is just many different ideas about God, the human condition, and what life is for. No real truth.

Through the prophet Isaiah, God says, **"He who blesses himself in the land shall bless himself by the God of truth, and he who takes an oath in the land shall swear by the God of truth"** (Isaiah 65:16 ESV). He is "the God of truth," for he is the source of truth, the arbiter of truth, and the one who holds people accountable for their denial of truth. This is why historically an oath to tell the truth in a courtroom concluded with, "so help me, God." A corollary to the fact that truth and God are synonymous is that God cannot lie. Listen to how the apostle Paul began his letter to Titus: **"Paul, a servant of God and an apostle of Jesus Christ to further the** faith of God's elect and their knowledge of the truth that leads to godliness—in the hope of eternal life, which God, who does not lie, promised before the beginning of time" (1:1,2). If God said it, that settles it. Here's another corollary: **"I the Lord do not change"** (Malachi 3:6). The God who does not lie does not go back on his word, does not change his mind or his truth. Divine truth, truth revealed by God, is changeless. Opinions change, cultural perspectives change, civil laws may change, but truth doesn't change. To know the truth, one must listen to God.

God has revealed himself and truth in his Word, the Bible. Jesus said it this way in his prayer to his Father before his crucifixion: **"Sanctify them by the truth; your word is truth"** (John 17:17). Christians for centuries have used several words to describe what it means that God's Word is truth. The term *verbally inspired* states that every word of the Bible was given by the Holy Spirit through prophets and apostles. Jesus, in fact, called the Holy Spirit **"the Spirit of truth"** (John 14:17). All of the Bible is God's Word. The word *inerrant* means that there are no errors in the Bible, no untruths. A parallel word is *infallible*. When critics of the Bible reject these descriptors, truth collapses like a house of cards and people are left without real certainty about much of anything.

To know the truth, one must listen to God.

Truth matters to God. In his trial before Pontius Pilate, Jesus said this: **"The reason I was born and came into the world is to testify to the truth. Everyone on the side of truth listens to me"** (John 18:37). Alongside Jesus' purpose to seek and save the lost is this mission statement: Jesus, God's Son, came to testify to divine truth. Many people remember the response of Pilate: **"What is truth?"** (John 18:38). That skepticism reflects what is left when people reject the Son of God; they have no expectation of ever learning the truth. To be on the side of truth is to listen to Jesus. Twenty-five times in the gospel of John, Jesus introduces an important statement with the expression, "I tell you the truth" (*Amen* in Greek). Shortly before his confrontation with Pilate, Jesus makes the claim, **"I am the way and the truth and the life. No one comes to the Father except through me"** (John 14:6). Apart from Jesus, people won't find the truth or the way to life with God. Ultimate truth is not discovered; it is revealed by the God who *IS* the truth.

Apart from Jesus, people won't find the truth.

The Bible doesn't make truth claims about specific political issues, cultural preferences, or economic systems. Nonetheless, what the Bible does say about right and wrong, about love and compassion, about truth and justice should guide Jesus followers in their attitudes and convictions about politics, culture, and economics. Micah 6:8 is a good example: **"He has shown you, O mortal, what is good. And what does the Lord require of you? To act justly and to love mercy and to walk humbly with your God."** Where the Bible makes no truth claims, Christians will be careful not to cloak their strongly held opinions with the mantle of truth. As dangerous as it is to deny truth, it may be equally dangerous to claim truth where God hasn't.

The Bible *does* make truth claims about the identity, nature, will, and promises of God. It *does* make truth claims about the origin, nature, purpose, and destiny of human beings. It *does* make truth claims about moral right and wrong, as well as the consequence of rebellion against God's moral will. And the Bible *does* make truth claims about the only way to be right with God, to have everlasting life with

God in Jesus. To reject or ignore these truth claims is to put oneself on the wrong side of God.

The most insidious lie that Satan has sold to contemporary culture is that there are many valid routes to God and truth, that no one religion has all the truth. If Islam and Hinduism and Christianity are equally true, then the word *truth* has no meaning, for the many different religions of the world are mutually contradictory. If all religions are sort of true, then no religions are really true. At the conclusion of his presentation to the "Evangelizing Postmoderns" seminar at Trinity Evangelical Divinity School in May 1998, Roy Clements offered a parable that can be paraphrased as what follows:

> *A traveler stood at a signpost, perplexed by the innumerable paths before him and intimidated by the mist that obscured everything beyond the first few feet of the paths. Some paths looked wide and straight, but who could tell? One seemed narrow and little traveled. The sign, weathered and illegible at important points, advertised a way to the fountain of truth. Alas, which way it pointed could no longer be determined.*

> *Three other wayfarers appeared as the first stood there. "Excuse me," the traveler said to one of the newcomers. "Can you show me the way to the fountain of truth?"*

> *"You don't believe that rubbish about a fountain of truth, do you?" the newcomer responded. "There is no truth. Make the best of where you are."*

> *The second wayfarer responded to the same query*

by saying, "Ah, who can know? I am an agnostic on the question of truth. One simply can't prove the issue. Just pick any path. I wouldn't presume to impose my ideas on you. Be open minded."

The third wayfarer smiled and said, "It is an unnecessary question. All roads lead to the fountain of truth. They only appear to go in different directions."

The traveler remained perplexed. His map showed only that there were dangerous cliffs in the region, and the mist seemed even thicker than before.

Then a fourth figure appeared out of the mist. He had come down the steep, narrow, and less-trodden trail. "Can you show me the way to the fountain of truth?" the man asked him.

"Indeed I can," came the reply. "The others were just guessing. They've never been to the fountain of truth. I live there. Follow me. I am the truth."

As the stranger extended his hand, the man noticed a nail print.

Will he take the hand offered him? Or will he decide that he likes life at the signpost, seemingly safe if not sure or meaningful? Maybe he fears that if he takes that hand, he will become a slave to the one who leads him. Can't he see? This is crucified truth. Crucified truth does not bully or coerce. This One invites: "Follow me. I am the Way and the Truth and the Life."

Think About It

What are the alternatives to believing that the Bible is verbally inspired and inerrant? Have you observed that a lesser view of the Bible inevitably leads to the denial of basic Christian teaching?

A consequence of biological evolution is sociological evolution—the idea that traditional convictions about marriage and religion, for example, are evolving to become better. What other changes in people's view of life are the result of the idea that evolution isn't restricted to biology?

Have you noticed changes in the way that people think about God? How does conventional wisdom or political correctness become a filter through which people hear God's Word?

The Truth Hurts

The self-esteem movement of the 1980s left us with participation trophies and grade inflation for American children, but also a lot of political correctness for adults. A recent example from a Midwestern city is no longer calling prisoners inmates, but rather residents, so as not to damage their self-esteem. Now, no one would contest that thinking well of oneself leads to greater success than thinking poorly of oneself. But there's an underlying assumption that should be examined. Secular humanism would have us believe that human beings are inherently good. In the face of rising crime rates and rampant corruption in business and government, people continue to hang on to this notion of inherent goodness.

People continue to hang on to this notion of inherent goodness.

The Bible has a different message. Quoting the psalmist David, the apostle Paul wrote, **"There is no one righteous, not even one; there is no one who understands; there is no one who seeks God. All have turned away, they have together become worthless; there is no one who does good, not even one. Their throats are open graves; their tongues practice deceit. The poison of vipers is on their lips. Their mouths are full of cursing and bitterness. Their feet are swift to shed blood; ruin and misery mark their ways, and the way of peace they do not know. There is no fear of God before their eyes"** (Romans 3:10-18). In Psalm 51 David said this: **"Surely I was sinful at birth, sinful from the time my mother conceived me"** (verse 5).

The truth hurts. Just as physical hurt is the body's message that something must be done, the psychological hurt of the Bible's message signals the need for intervention. Ignoring or denying the capacity of every human being for wickedness is destructive for the future of society. Rationalizing away excesses of evil invites more evil. Defunding the police and decriminalizing wrongdoing seem like ignoring the truth about human nature. After the killing of nine people in San Jose in May 2021, Gavin Newsom, the governor of California, said, "What the hell is wrong with us?" There is an answer to that question, but the truth hurts.

A line from William Ernest Henley's poem *Invictus* that has been oft repeated says, "I am the master of my fate, I am the captain of my soul." A current version says, "If you can imagine it, you can do it; if you can think it, you can be it." Sounds good, but is it true? For every person who realized the success story he imagined, there are many frustrated people left to blame others or circumstances for their failures. Blaming self would be damaging to the psyche, and blaming the delusionary promises that set people up for frustration somehow doesn't occur to them. Can we control our own lives? Can we achieve what we want with positive thinking and hard work? There is some truth in this, but there is a greater truth that stands in the way of self-glorification.

The apostle Peter wrote, **"But there were also false prophets among the people, just as there will be false teachers among you. They will secretly introduce destructive heresies, even denying the sovereign Lord who bought them"** (2 Peter 2:1). God is sovereign. That means he is in control of our lives and our world. He makes decisions that cannot be overruled. He determines the boundaries of our future and can alter the course of our lives. It is a destructive heresy to attribute to human beings the authority and power of God. God is sovereign, not human beings. The truth hurts.

From the time we are children, we learn to say, "It isn't fair." We don't always get what we deserve. Laws aren't applied equitably. Sometimes wealth isn't earned honestly. People die before their time (whatever that means). Life isn't fair. Wise Solomon wrote, **"There is something else meaningless that occurs on earth: the righteous who get what the wicked deserve, and the wicked who get what the righteous deserve"** (Ecclesiastes 8:14). Maybe you've heard the philosophical argument stated this way: Why do bad things happen to good people? What you haven't heard is a coherent answer. In the Bible, Job verges on demanding an answer to the question from God, and God's response sends Job cringing in penitent silence (Job 38–42). Reality hurts. Truth hurts. Not only are we not in control of our lives and destinies, but we can't even comprehend why some things happen.

There is a still more painful truth. We are accountable for our wrongs. **"It is written: 'As surely as I live,' says the Lord, 'every knee will bow before me; every tongue will acknowledge God.' So then, each of us will give an account of ourselves to God"** (Romans 14:11,12). While we may be able to keep our sins hidden from others and we may escape

People tell themselves lies because the truth hurts.

punishment for our wrongs here and now, there is an eternal reckoning. There's nowhere to hide, no defense to offer. **"For all have sinned and fall short of the glory of God"** (Romans 3:23). Jesus said: **"Do not be afraid of those who kill the body but cannot kill the soul. Rather, be afraid of the One who can destroy both soul and body in hell"** (Matthew 10:28). People tell themselves lies because the truth hurts.

Think About It

How might public policy change if people accepted the truth about the sinful nature of human beings?

Read the account of the tower of Babel in Genesis 11:1-9. What was so bad about this tower of secular humanism? Do societies still build metaphorical towers?

Are there truths about you that hurt enough that you'd rather not think about them, let alone air them?

The Truth Will Set You Free

Nearly everyone has heard this sentence: The truth will set you free. But far fewer have understood the sentence in its context. Here's what Jesus said: **"If you hold to my teaching, you are really my disciples. Then you will know the truth, and the truth will set you free"** (John 8:31,32). Jesus' teaching is the truth, and holding on to that teaching is the key to freedom. Disciples of Jesus, people who follow Jesus and learn from Jesus, people who have committed themselves to Jesus, will know the truth. Knowing the truth is essential to being freed by that truth. That takes serious study. A vague idea of what Jesus taught won't cut it. Good feelings about Jesus won't matter. Freedom rests in knowing Jesus, following Jesus, growing in an understanding of Jesus' teaching.

Freedom, in Jesus' words, isn't a license to do what you please, as though you can be free of moral restraints and God-ordained authority. Real freedom isn't the right to say what you feel, as if Jesus were simply endorsing the First Amendment to the U. S. Constitution. Too many people have cited Jesus' words as support for rejecting social standards or advocating cultural reforms. What Jesus meant when he promised that knowing the truth will set you free centers in our relationship with God through Jesus.

Revelation 1:5 focuses attention on **"Jesus Christ, who is the faithful witness, the firstborn from the dead, and the ruler of the kings of the earth . . . who loves us and has freed us from our sins by his blood."** Sin is like a ball and chain that limits us, like a cell imprisoning us. Jesus freed us from our sin with the blood he shed for us. Sin separates us from our God, leaving us in despair about our present and in fear of our future. Jesus freed us from that fear and despair by restoring us to a right relationship with our God with the blood he shed at Calvary. There are many dimensions to the freedom that is ours in the truth Jesus gives us.

To understand what our sin has done to hurt others and violate God's will is to experience guilt. Unresolved guilt drives us away from the person against whom we've sinned, whether human or divine, and that alienation robs us of inner peace. To realize that our sin is not a one-off and that our human nature is deeply flawed and inclined toward more sin can produce shame. Shame isolates us from others and from God; it robs us of a sense of worth and hope. This psychological impact of sin produces insecurity, and that insecurity leads us to seek the approval of others—sometimes at great moral cost to our souls. But forgiveness removes guilt and dispels shame. Once we are more right with God, we can have healthy interactions with others. Romans 3:24 assures us: **"All are justified freely by his grace through the redemption that came by Christ Jesus."** *Justified* is a courtroom term declaring us not guilty. Jesus paid the penalty our sin deserved, and we are set free.

Sin creates a fear of death and of hell. People may try to convince themselves that there's nothing after death, that hell is just some religious leverage for making people behave. Or they may hope that they're good enough to make the cut if there is an afterlife. At least they haven't killed anyone, they think. Still, the fear lingers; and in a hospital room, with monitors beeping a mortal dirge, the happy talk dissipates. Regret brings tears. Fear dominates thought. What if? Well, Jesus freed us from the fear of death and hell because he endured death and hell for us. After an agonizing tour through good intentions but bad behaviors in Romans chapter 7, the apostle Paul concludes, **"There is now no condemnation for those who are in Christ Jesus, because through Christ Jesus the law of the Spirit who gives life has set you free from the law of sin and death"** (Romans 8:1,2). *That* is the truth Jesus provides, Jesus and no one else.

No matter how affluent and healthy you are, no matter how successful, anxiety can interrupt your sleep and plague your waking hours with worry. Maybe all this will end in misfortune. Maybe life will catch up with you and the other shoe will drop. How can you protect your kids? It's bad enough to know that you aren't in control of your life. Much worse is wondering if the God who is in control doesn't like you. Sin is every reason for him not to like you. Jesus frees us from that anxiety by reassuring us that our God loves us, that he loves to bless us, that in the worst of times he will be there to carry us through. The psalmist put it this way: **"The Lord is with me; I will not be afraid. What can mere mortals do to me?"** (Psalm 118:6). St. Paul draws a logical conclusion from the fact that God's Son gave his life for us: **"He who did not spare his own Son, but gave him up for us all—how will he not also, along with him, graciously give us all things?"** (Romans 8:32).

For too many people, religion is a chore, rituals to observe and rules to keep. It doesn't feel like freedom but rather duty and drudgery. Behind this is the notion that somehow you have

The truth Jesus teaches frees us from dull religion.

to do stuff to put God on your side, or at least to get him off your back. Even Christians who've learned that God's forgiveness is free, that grace covers them and God loves them, can still turn their religion into a tradition and an obligation. The truth Jesus teaches frees us from dull religion. We don't *have to* do stuff for God;

we *get to* do stuff for God. Shortly before his crucifixion, Jesus said to his disciples, **"I have told you this so that my joy may be in you and that your joy may be complete. . . . I no longer call you servants, because a servant does not know his master's business. Instead, I have called you friends, for everything that I learned from my Father I have made known to you"** (John 15:11–15). We have been set free to enjoy our relationship with God. We are Jesus' friends, co-workers in his mission on earth.

In a world lacking honesty, people have a healthy fear of scammers, people who will steal our identity and our reputation, our money and our security. The more money means to you, the more susceptible to scammers you may be. More serious are those who would scam us with ideas that lead us away from God and into fear or anger or false hopes. They could be teachers or preachers. They may be blogs and podcasts. They prey on our uncertainties and suspicions. Who can you trust? How do you know what to believe? Jesus frees us from gullibility by giving us truth that is the touchstone against which to measure all ideas and claims.

The God of love frees us to love. That's important because what keeps people from loving others is the fear that they'll be taken advantage of. Loving others makes one vulnerable; unconditional love can get you hurt. We can't give generously if we're afraid that we won't have enough. We can't help if we're caught up in our busyness. Life lived for oneself is a kind of prison. Jesus sets us free with the truth. The apostle John wrote, **"We love because he first loved us"** (1 John 4:19).

There are so many limiters and so many inhibitors to life. There are so many things that can keep us from enjoying a life that is fulfilling. Jesus frees us from all that. The truth will set you free.

Think About It

Identify some of the false freedoms that entice people today to abandon moral moorings.

Why do we sometimes think of our relationship with God as a burden or a guilt trip? What are we missing in those times?

How are addictions a form of spiritual slavery? What does the gospel offer to help people caught in an addiction?

Half-Truths and Big Lies

"That may be your truth, but it's not my truth."

This is a confusion of categories and an attempt to redefine *truth*. A definition of *truth* is *"what corresponds to fact or reality."* "Your truth isn't my truth" redefines truth as a subjective opinion or personal viewpoint. If truth is no more than the way a person thinks or feels about a subject, there can be no objective and absolute truth. Then facts don't matter, and reality is whatever you perceive it to be. People who confuse opinion with truth wouldn't likely claim that 2 + 2 = 4 is just one person's truth, while another person could legitimately believe that 2 + 2 = 5. They wouldn't argue that the law of gravity doesn't work for everybody. So math and hard science can remain in the realm of fact, but truth moves to another realm? Truth in a postmodern world is relegated to a category in which people can have their own **Truth belongs in the category of fact, not opinion.** cultural, moral, and religious opinions and pretend that these are truth. Radio host Kurt Andersen aptly said, "You are entitled to your own opinions, but you are not entitled to your own facts." Truth belongs in the category of fact, not opinion.

This generation has created virtual reality, a realm that is somewhere between reality and perception. Reality then becomes an experience rather than a fact. A Chinese communist can have a different reality than an American democrat. A poor African has a different reality than a wealthy European. And a militant atheist has a different reality than a Bible-believing Christian. Here are a couple of dictionary definitions for *reality*: 1) "the world or the state of things as they actually exist, as opposed to an idealistic or notional idea of them"; 2) "the state or quality of having existence or substance." That sounds nothing like what the claim "your truth isn't my truth" argues. Again, the word *reality* is redefined from something concrete to what is felt or experienced. Truth becomes whatever "reality" you choose to accept. Think about it; have people today lost touch with reality? That is a definition of insanity.

So why does this matter? If truth is personal or subjective, God has no say on the subject. In fact, if God is whoever or whatever a person thinks him/her to be, God is just a concept. Or maybe he's a figment of human imagination. Then, of course, he can't issue moral imperatives for which human beings are accountable. He can't offer real forgiveness and an eternal existence of perfect joy beyond this world. Contemporary culture views truth as *relative*, but relative to what? When there is no fixed point of truth and reality, there is nothing a person can bank on. When nothing is really real, all meaning in life is lost. That's the inescapable conclusion that people would like to escape.

You may recall the confrontation between Elijah and the prophets of the pagan deity Baal. Here's what Elijah said: **"How long will you waver between two opinions? If the Lord is God, follow him; but if Baal is God, follow him"** (1 Kings 18:21). The fire God sent from heaven decided the issue. God isn't an opinion. He's a fact. He's the Truth. To describe God and his Word as a personal "truth," an opinion separated from fact, is to deny God entirely.

Think About It

What are some of the arenas in which people want to make truth a personal rather than an objective thing?

In ancient history, a conquering nation often absorbed the gods and myths of the nations they conquered into their own religious outlook. Has America done something similar in its relationship with Islam?

Can there be "personal truths" that lie outside the realm of biblical truth? Should we use the term *truth* for these?

"We all have a bit of the truth. No one has the whole truth."

That's certainly non-offensive. According to this politically correct statement, no matter how intelligent you are, no matter what your politics or religion, we are all in the same boat when it comes to truth; and that boat is sinking, logically. Think about it. If you have some of the truth but not all of it, how do you know that what you think to be true is actually your "bit of the truth"? You are more likely misguided than correct in your beliefs if you only have a bit of the truth. If we all have a bit of the truth, we also all lack most of the truth. It's difficult to trust yourself, let alone anyone else, if truth comes in little parcels distributed among lots of people with no way of knowing who has what pieces of truth. Apart from an objective standard of truth, outside of yourself, there is no way of knowing whether what you think or believe is actually true. To say that we all have a bit of the truth is not only non-offensive; it is nonsensical if truth is to be taken seriously.

That no one has the whole truth does not mean that there is not a "whole truth." Human beings may be incapable of perceiving the whole truth, but an all-knowing God can easily possess the whole truth. If that God reveals the whole truth to human beings, then they can access the whole truth. There are potentially at least three different ways to arrive at truth: by intuition, through reason, or by revelation. As an example, consider the moral judgment that killing others is wrong. One could arrive at that judgment by intuition. In other words, it just seems or feels wrong to kill other people. Of course, it may also seem that some people deserve to die; so how sure can a person be about the morality of murder? One could conclude rationally that it is wrong to kill others. After all, if everyone killed others, there would be no human beings left. Of course, the evolutionary reasoning called "survival of the fittest" would lead to the conclusion that killing the weak, those with intellectual or physical disabilities, is essential to the advancement of the human species. Adolph Hitler only actualized what eugenics argued rationally in early 20th-century America. Intuition and reason are inadequate avenues for arriving at truth. When "thou shalt not kill" is a moral truth revealed by a sovereign God, that is a "whole truth." Thinking or feeling has nothing to do with it.

Intuition and reason are inadequate avenues for arriving at truth.

You've heard that a little knowledge is a dangerous thing. Well, a bit of truth is also a dangerous thing. Believing that mushrooms are a delicious addition to your cooking, without knowing that some mushrooms are deadly, is a dangerous thing. Believing that a parachute will land you safely after exiting an airplane is a bit of the truth. If you don't know what a rip cord is, a bit of the truth could kill you. More to the point, acknowledging that there is a supreme being is a bit of the truth one can arrive at by observing creation or reflecting on one's own desire to survive death. But not knowing who that supreme being is or how to get on his good side leaves a person with doubts and fears and ultimately leaves that person outside God's presence eternally. In Acts chapter 17, the apostle Paul acknowledges the "bit of the truth" that Athenian philosophers had and affirms that they were very religious. But all that religiosity achieved was a pantheon of nature deities and an altar to an "unknown God." The Athenians were covering their bases with that altar, but their religious reasoning could only arrive at uncertainty. The true God can only be known as he reveals himself. The revelation of himself in the person of God's Son, Jesus, is the missing truth that the apostle explained to the Athenians. It's not the bits of truth you have but the truth you don't have that can kill you.

The Pharisees of Jesus' day had many bits of truth, truth revealed by God through Moses and the Prophets. What they had missed was the central truth that brought their bits of truth to a complete whole. They understood the identity and nature of God, as well as his moral will for their lives. But in their self-righteous efforts to earn God's favor, they added to God's moral will a set of religious rules that made them look good and minimized their failures to obey the very heart of God's moral will—love. Because they missed the promises of God, from Abraham through the prophets, they failed to see in Jesus the Savior who kept God's moral will perfectly in their stead and died for them as the price of their moral failures. The very laws of God became bits of truth that kept the Pharisees from recognizing the whole truth.

There are countless ways to suppress the truth, to distort the truth, and to dismiss the truth. Every generation must contend with fine-sounding arguments like "everyone has a bit of the truth." Unpack the arguments and they prove hollow. God gave us something better in passages like these from Isaiah 59: **"Our offenses are ever with us, and we acknowledge our iniquities: rebellion and treachery against the Lord, turning our backs on our God, inciting revolt and oppression, uttering lies our hearts have conceived. So justice is driven back, and righteousness stands at a distance; truth has stumbled in the streets, honesty cannot enter. Truth is nowhere to be found, and whoever shuns evil becomes a prey. The Lord looked and was displeased. . . . So his own arm achieved salvation for him, and his own righteousness sustained him. He put on righteousness as his breastplate, and the helmet of sal-**

vation on his head; he put on the garments of vengeance and wrapped himself in zeal as in a cloak. . . . 'The Redeemer will come to Zion, to those in Jacob who repent of their sins,' declares the Lord. 'As for me, this is my covenant with them,' says the Lord. 'My Spirit, who is on you, will not depart from you, and my words that I have put in your mouth will always be on your lips, on the lips of your children and on the lips of their descendants—from this time on and forever,' says the Lord" (verses 12-17,20,21).

Think About It

Do you see Jesus in those verses from Isaiah 59? Do you see the reason Jesus came as well? Is life any different today from Isaiah's day?

Political correctness avoids telling anyone that they are wrong. Point out some dangers in that approach to handling truth.

Half-truths, like "bits of truth," are a way of hiding from people an accurate picture of reality. Give examples of half-truths that are intended to keep people in the dark.

"It's not a lie if you believe it to be true."

That sounds nonsensical. Believing that I'm a rock star won't make it true. Believing that COVID-19 was just a myth won't keep me from getting really sick. So why would people even say something like, "It's not a lie if you believe it to be true"? One reason is that truth has been altered, from meaning what is factual or what really happened to "how I see it." Truth, for too many people, has become a perception. The other reason is that people don't want to be accountable for their lies. Politicians may lie in order to make themselves look better or to make their agendas more acceptable. They are willing to alter facts to fit their message. They may well believe that the way they remember things is the way things actually happened, because self-deception is very real. They may believe that it is in the best interest of the populace to accept the lie rather than deal with the truth. Politicians are not alone. Common folks lie to escape blame or to provide themselves honorable motives. After a while, we may begin to believe that we were only trying to do the right thing, only seeking the best for others. So what is a lie?

A lie has historically meant something that didn't really happen or didn't happen the way a person wants to spin it. A lie is a distortion of the facts, a statement that doesn't square with reality. Interestingly, a current definition of a lie adds the element of intent or motive. Lying is *deliberately* deceiving someone, *intentionally* conveying a false impression. Truth takes a hit if an untruth isn't a lie unless the person speaking it intends to deceive. And who can determine the intent of the liar since motives are hidden in the heart. Redefining a lie is not new. Ethical philosophy has made lying moral if the intent is to not hurt someone else's feelings. When a woman asks, "Does this dress make me look fat?" the sensitive answer isn't truth but, "No, of course not, honey." Okay, so that's not a big deal. On a deeper level, lying to prevent harm to others is portrayed as morally correct. When an abusive neighbor asks where his wife went, the right thing, then, is to lie. Or is it? There is an alternative: refusing to answer. But that puts oneself at risk. Maybe we convince ourselves that our lie is to prevent hurting others when the reality is that we don't want to be hurt ourselves. We can find good motives for bad words. When the Bible says, **"Do not lie to each other"** (Colossians 3:9), it isn't asking us to look within to determine our motives or look outside ourselves to calculate likely outcomes. Redefining a lie is also redefining the truth.

King Saul knew how to rationalize his willful disobedience. He may even have believed that the way he reinterpreted God's command was acceptable, that the lie he told the prophet Samuel wasn't really a lie because he believed his own spin. God wasn't impressed. Here's how the Old Testament relates the story:

Samuel confronted Saul: **"Why did you not obey the** Lord**? Why did you pounce on the plunder and do evil in the eyes of the** Lord**?"**

"But I did obey the Lord**," Saul said. "I went on the mission the** Lord **assigned me. I completely destroyed the Amalekites and brought back Agag their king. The soldiers took sheep and cattle from the plunder, the best of what was devoted to God, in order to sacrifice them to the** Lord **your God at Gilgal."**

But Samuel replied: "Does the Lord **delight in burnt offerings and sacrifices as much**

as in obeying the Lord? To obey is better than sacrifice, and to heed is better than the fat of rams. For rebellion is like the sin of divination, and arrogance like the evil of idolatry. Because you have rejected the word of the Lord, he has rejected you as king." (1 Samuel 15:19-23)

Whether we deliberately lie or we convince ourselves that we're only bending the truth to avoid hurting someone's feelings, whether we actually believe the lie or know we are lying, our intentions and delusions don't alter reality. Rationalizing wrong is a road to spiritual suicide. Confessing our sin to God assures forgiveness, and that forgiveness can give us the courage to be honest with others, no matter what.

Think About It

Here's what God said to Jeremiah about lies told to the people of Judah: **"A horrible and shocking thing has happened in the land: The prophets prophesy lies, the priests rule by their own authority, and my people love it this way. But what will you do in the end?"** (Jeremiah 5:30,31). Which was worse, that prophets lied or that the people wanted to hear the lies? Do you think that people today want to hear the truth?

Do you think people actually convince themselves that a lie is the truth? How does that happen?

The position of some ethical philosophers is that a lie is withholding the truth from someone who is owed the truth. What problem can you see with that definition?

"It's my body. I can do what I want with it."

Sure, if you want to get a tattoo or body piercing, if you want to dye your hair green, go for it. But that's not what people mean with the claim above. The issue is whether you have an absolute right to do what you want with your body. Actually, the government says no, you don't. You don't have the legal right to shoot up heroin or drive drunk. You are required to wear a seat belt when driving. You can't use your fist to punch someone's lights out. The local school board can tell you that you have to wear a mask to prevent the spread of a pandemic. The government passes laws to protect you from yourself, but the bigger reason for such laws is to protect others from what you may want to do with your body. But that's still not what people are talking about typically with the claim above.

If you are carrying another person inside your body, doing what you want with your body may impinge on the health and safety of that child. Seeing the struggles of a crack cocaine baby or a child suffering with fetal alcohol syndrome should convince you that a mother does not have the right to do what she wants with her body. If that makes sense to you, then the idea of killing the baby in your womb should seem absolutely abhorrent. And yet, abortion is legal, based on a court's ruling that abortion falls under a vague constitutional right to privacy. For a time, proponents of abortion argued that a fetus was not a life. That argument has been largely abandoned in the face of overwhelming medical science. Instead, the claim is that the life in the womb is not a person. What defines a person seems more than a bit arbitrary. Another claim sets the bar for continuing life in the womb at viability. Can the child live without what the mother's womb supplies? Of course, the baby is no more able to live without a mother after birth than before, and independence as a definition of viability is a slippery slope toward euthanasia. A more honest argument has pitted the quality of life against the fact of life. If a child is unwanted, impaired by a disability, or likely facing hunger and poverty, wouldn't it be better that the child not be born? That argument is based on multiple assumptions about the future as well as an arbitrary standard of what makes life worth living. Ultimately, is there a woman's "right to choose" that trumps a baby's right to life? The heated debate goes on in our culture, but even a champion for women's rights ought to wrestle with the moral dilemma of acting in uncertainty. If there's even just a possibility that abortion is killing a baby, how can a person go ahead with it?

The other arena in which people maintain the right to do what they want with their body is sex. That this is not an absolute right is apparent because rape and other forms of sexual assault are felonies. Using my body to harm another person is clearly wrong, and pedophilia is the most egregious example of just how wrong. The issue is more than age. From a legal perspective, the issue is consent. Is sex among consenting people a right? What if psychological manipulation produced that consent? What if an extramarital affair harms a spouse who certainly did not consent to the affair? How about the children affected by adultery and subsequent divorce? And what about the unintended consequences, emotional and physical, that may result from sex outside of marriage? There's more to the subject than merely the claim that "I can do what I want with my body."

More important than what is legal or logical is the question of whether something is morally right. Not *can* you do what you want with your body, but *should* you do what you want. What is your responsibility toward others in what you do with your body? Can your wants drive your actions in willful selfishness? The answer to such questions is difficult when moral right and wrong are decided by societal consensus or individual preference, if there is no absolute right and wrong decided above and beyond conflicting opinions. God has something to say about this.

That God is the Creator doesn't simply mean he got life started and then sat back to watch what happens. In Psalm 139:13,14 David states clearly that each of us is the unique creation of God as he directs genetic biology in the womb: **"For you created my inmost being; you knit me together in my mother's womb. I praise you because I am fearfully and wonderfully made; your works are wonderful."** The God who created life has the right to determine the rules for life, a right far exceeding that of individuals and what they want to do with their bodies. There is peril in defying God's moral will, here and hereafter.

Listen to what the apostle Paul says about what you do with your body as he wrote to an oversexed culture: **"It is God's will that you should be sanctified: that you should avoid sexual immorality; that** *each of you should learn to control your own body in a way that is holy and honorable,* **not in passionate lust like the pagans, who do not know God; and that in this matter no one should wrong or take advantage of a brother or sister. The Lord will punish all those who commit such sins, as we told you and warned you before. For God did not call us to be impure, but to live a holy life. Therefore, anyone who rejects this instruction does not reject a human being but God"** (1 Thessalonians 4:3-8).

Can you do what you want with your body? Does your body belong to you alone? St. Paul argues that there is a higher claim on a Christian's body: **"Flee from sexual immorality. All other sins a person commits are outside the** body, but whoever sins sexually, sins against their own body. Do you not know that your bodies are temples of the Holy Spirit, who is in you, whom you have received from God? *You are not your own; you were bought at a price. Therefore honor God with your bodies"* (1 Corinthians 6:18–20).

Enough said.

Think About It

Can and *should* are two different questions. Think of other arenas in life where *should* trumps *can*. The problem lies with who determines the *should*.

How does sex education look different in a Christian school from a public school?

False arguments often pit two extremes against each other. One example is arguing that it would be better to abort a baby rather than have it born unwanted and raised with abuse. Are those really the only two possibilities?

"The heart wants what the heart wants."

Of course it does, but is that a good thing? Common advice to people making a career decision or a marriage proposal has often been, "Follow your heart." That's not such bad counsel. A career that matches what you are good at and enjoy doing will likely stimulate an emotional response. Following your head may make more practical sense, but you may grow to hate your job. Of course, a rush of excitement that is not tempered by a realistic assessment of what taking that job may mean could end in heartache. Romantic attraction means experiencing a sense of euphoria in the company of the person you're dating, a comfortability with your "soul mate," deeply missing the person when you're not together. Marriage isn't a rational transaction. However, failing to think through what living with the person you love will mean is responsible for a lot of early divorces. Feelings change. Emotion and intuition are important aspects of the decisions we make, but without the common sense of reason, following your heart can end badly.

A century ago, "follow your heart" would not likely be the kind of advice given. "Think it through," "weigh the pros and cons," and "look at the long term" are the principles one might expect to hear. What changed? Postmodern culture devalued reason and logic in favor of emotion and experience. Hard and fast moral boundaries gave way to relative or flexible assessments of what's right. So 50 years ago the advice became, "If it feels good, do it." The theme song for the 1970s TV show *Happy Days* included this lyric: "Feels so right, you can't be wrong." And that leads to the contemporary expression: "The heart wants what the heart wants."

What is meant by "the heart"? Feelings, desires, intuition. In Bible times the heart stood for loyalty and commitment chiefly, something stronger and more settled than a feeling. "Gut feelings" placed the seat of intuition in one's intestines rather than the heart. Think about the difference in a couple saying to each other at their engagement, "I give you my heart." That is meant to convey commitment, not merely a feeling. "The heart wants what the heart wants" sounds more selfish, more momentary. Desire and commitment are very different things.

Can you trust your heart? Several generations after the fall into sin, God had this assessment of the human heart: **"The Lord saw how great the wickedness of the human race had become on the earth, and that every inclination of the thoughts of the human heart was only evil all the time"** (Genesis 6:5). The Bible teaches that even Christians have a human nature inclined toward sin. The problem with life is that people's inclinations aren't always good. What the heart wants may not be healthy for the soul. The heart's wants may be harmful to others. Listen to Jeremiah 17:9: **"The heart is deceitful above all things and beyond cure. Who can understand it?"** You can be tricked by your feelings into thinking that bad is good. Sinful desires can overrule what you know to be true. "The heart wants what the heart wants" is a rationalization for self-centered desires. It suggests that you can't help yourself, that you have to follow your feelings. It will even turn wants into needs, as though you just have to do what you feel like doing. That's the devil's lie. We can say no to our hearts.

The heart is not a moral compass; it's merely a desire. Desire needs boundaries. Emotion needs guidance. Solomon, upon taking the throne in Israel, prayed, **"Give your servant a discerning heart to govern your people and to** distinguish between right and wrong" (1 Kings 3:9). The heart requires the boundaries of truth, and truth guides the heart with the Word of God. King David, after confessing his sin and seeking God's forgiveness, offered this prayer: "Create in me a pure heart, O God, and renew a steadfast spirit within me" (Psalm 51:10). And again: "Teach me your way, LORD, that I may rely on your faithfulness; give me an undivided heart, that I may fear your name" (Psalm 86:11). When the heart wants what God wants, life is good. But God has to change hearts and fill hearts and direct hearts in order for human hearts to align with God's heart. Proverbs 4:23 offers sound advice: "Above all else, guard your heart, for everything you do flows from it."

Jesus told the parable of the lost son (Luke 15) to illustrate what happens when "the heart wants what the heart wants." Rebelling against the values of his father, a young man takes his father's money and spends it on the lusts of his wayward heart. When the money is gone, so are the friends he partied with. He is left empty and despairing. Temporary pleasure ended in physical and emotional disaster. But the real point of the story is the father's forgiveness and restoration of his son. Our God doesn't just make the rules that make life worth living. He forgives penitent sinners when they break those rules. Because Jesus endured the price of our sinning, God takes away our sin and renews in us hearts that treasure his will.

Think About It

Second Samuel chapters 13–18 are dedicated to the life of Absalom. Read chapter 13 to see what started a calamitous sequence of falling dominoes because "the heart wants what the heart wants."

Think about what it says when schools distribute condoms. Is sex among the unmarried inevitable, unavoidable? At what point does recognizing the power of lust become legitimizing the power of lust?

In practical terms, what does it mean to "guard your heart"? What's the strategy?

"You owe it to yourself to do what makes you happy."

If that means a glass of wine after a hard day or a long weekend to celebrate the completion of a big project, yes, maybe you owe that happiness to yourself. If that means finding a job that you enjoy or a hobby that helps you unwind, then yes, that makes sense. If doing what makes you happy comes at the expense of your family's happiness or crosses a moral line, well, what kind of debt do you think you owe yourself?

The Declaration of Independence guarantees Americans "the pursuit of happiness," not the experience of happiness. Interestingly, the Declaration of Independence does not define happiness or proscribe the parameters of a legitimate pursuit of happiness. Happiness is not an inalienable right. The government doesn't owe you happiness, nor does your boss. Maybe your family owes you some happiness. But why do you owe yourself happiness? Is it because you're a good person or because you contribute to the welfare of your community? Or is it just because you exist and maybe no one else cares much about your happiness?

What has changed is the notion that self is the priority.

There are a lot of things that we owe. We owe obedience to the government, at least up to the point where the government requires what God forbids. We have a responsibility to our families and employers, organizations we join, and promises we make. Those are legitimate "debts." Where does owing yourself happiness fit into the bigger picture of your life? A few generations ago, consensus thinking would have placed your happiness well below what was owed to your family and your job. Doing the right thing was valued above feeling happy. What has changed is the notion that self is the priority. "Take care of number one" is a slogan that expresses this emphasis on self. The apostle Paul has a different take on this subject: **"Owe no one anything, except to love each other"** (Romans 13:8 ESV). What is owed is selfless love for others.

What is happiness? Philosophers in ancient history used the Latin term *summum bonum* or highest good for the goal and organizing principle of life. Happiness was one way of defining this *summum bonum*, but philosophers disagreed about what happiness was. For the Epicureans, happiness meant the experience of pleasure and the absence of pain. For Stoics, happiness came with accepting your circumstances and making the best of them. Aristotle taught that happiness was the pursuit of virtue. Current culture seems to side with the Epicureans, but the Epicureans recognized that selfishness produces *un*happiness. If owing yourself happiness is a self-centered view of life, happiness may be temporary pleasure followed by a lot of pain.

If "you owe it to yourself to do what makes you happy" is the reason for an extramarital affair, don't expect a happy ending. If owing yourself happiness explains why you quit your job and blew your life savings in Las Vegas, there may well be some unhappy consequences. When people define their happiness only in terms of sensory pleasure, such happiness cannot last. When there are no moral boundaries to a person's happiness, other people are bound to be hurt. When my happiness is at odds with the happiness of others, doing what makes me happy is a form of bullying.

As you might expect, the Bible weighs in on the subject of happiness. Psalm 144:15 says, **"Happy *are* the people whose God *is* the Lord!"** (NKJV). Proverbs 3:13 adds, **"Happy *is* the man *who* finds wisdom"** (NKJV). Real happiness, according to the Bible, is not found in pleasure seeking but in seeking wisdom and a relationship with God. But the Bible has a more counterintuitive view of happiness in the words of Jesus. The Greek word translated "blessed" (*makarios*) in the Beatitudes (Matthew 5:3-12) can also be translated "happy." More than one author has called the Beatitudes "the be happy attitudes." Here's what the Beatitudes look like with that translation:

> "Happy are the poor in spirit, for theirs is the kingdom of heaven. Happy are those who mourn, for they will be comforted. Happy are the meek, for they will inherit the earth. Happy are those who hunger and thirst for righteousness, for they will be filled. Happy are the merciful, for they will be shown mercy. Happy are the pure in heart, for they will see God. Happy are the peacemakers, for they will be called children of God. Happy are those who are persecuted because of righteousness, for theirs is the kingdom of heaven. Happy are you when people insult you, persecute you and falsely say all kinds of evil against you because of me. Rejoice and be glad, because great is your reward in heaven, for in the same way they persecuted the prophets who were before you."

Happiness, in Jesus' view, means humility before God and others, not self-centeredness. Happiness is not seeking your own pleasure but deferring to others. It is looking for opportunities to do the right thing and rejoicing in the forgiveness that covers all the wrong things. Happiness is not winning arguments but bringing people together around the truth. And there is happiness in suffering for what is right and looking to eternity for vindication. There can be happiness in the midst of suffering. The apostle Peter understood what Jesus meant. He wrote, **"But even if you should suffer for what is right, you are** [*happy*]**"** (1 Peter 3:14). And again, **"If you are insulted because of the name of Christ, you are** [*happy*]**, for the Spirit of glory and of God rests on you"** (1 Peter 4:14).

Perhaps we can restate the case. You owe it to your God to do what makes you truly happy. And that will make God happy.

Think About It

What are some things that you thought would make you happy but turned out to leave you feeling disappointed and empty?

When you see eternal life with Jesus as the *summum bonum* or greatest good, how does temporary happiness look different?

What is the difference among pleasure, happiness, and joy? Which do you owe yourself? Who owes you any of these?

"You have to learn to love yourself."

If that means narcissistic self-centeredness, it's a lie. The world doesn't need any more people who exaggerate their importance, indulge their fantasies, and take advantage of others. But the opposite extreme, self-hatred, is equally destructive. People who put themselves down typically look for others to build them up, and that neediness is exhausting. Self-loathing leads to low achievement and sometimes self-harm. Is there a healthy way to understand loving yourself?

In answering a question about the greatest commandment, Jesus said, **"'Love the Lord your God with all your heart and with all your soul and with all your mind.' This is the first and greatest commandment. And the second is like it: 'Love your neighbor as yourself'"** (Matthew 22:37-39). We *are* to love ourselves. It's the basis for loving others. The word *as* suggests that we should love our neighbor as much as we love ourselves. It also indicates loving others in the same way that we love ourselves. If we love ourselves more than we love others, we will turn inward and become self-indulgent; we will tend to use others to satisfy our own emotional needs. If we don't love ourselves, we will turn our self-hatred outward and mistreat others.

Loving God wholeheartedly is the prerequisite for proper love.

If self-love is expressed by cultivating habits that are healthy and attitudes that are positive, loving others will take the same form. There is more in what Jesus said. Loving God wholeheartedly is the prerequisite for proper love for self and others. If we are not committed to God above all else, our love for self and others will be shallow and misguided. Here's how the apostle John put it: **"We love because he first** loved us. Whoever claims to love God yet hates a brother or sister is a liar. For whoever does not love their brother and sister, whom they have seen, cannot love God, whom they have not seen" (1 John 4:19,20).

There are good reasons to love ourselves. God is our Creator. He has given us the personalities and talents that he determined, the physical characteristics and the mental capacity we have. To demean ourselves is to disrespect our Creator. As the bumper sticker reads: "I'm OK. God doesn't make junk." God is also our Redeemer. In spite of our sinning, he loves us; and to answer our sinning, he sent his Son, Jesus, to pay the price of our forgiveness. God wants us to spend forever with him. Self-hatred denies everything that Jesus' death on a cross accomplished for us. Christians believe that the Holy Spirit works on them and with them to grow faith and develop character. Another bumper sticker reads: "Be patient with me. God's not finished with me yet." It is not egotistical to appreciate what God has done with you. It is healthy self-image to recognize the blessings you enjoy and the possibilities that lie ahead because you are God's unique creation.

The Bible also gives reasons not to love ourselves too much. Ever since Adam and Eve rebelled against God and opposed his will, human beings have been born with a sinful human nature. Adam and Eve's first child, Cain, expressed that self-centered nature when he said, **"Am I my brother's keeper?"** (Genesis 4:9). Sinful human nature pits self against God and exalts self over others. Self-glorifying replaces God-glorifying. Pride uses others to make self look good. Sinful human nature competes with others rather than cooperates with others. It compares self with others instead of appreciating how we complement each other with our different gifts and personalities. Psalm 58:3 assesses human nature this way: **"Even from birth the wicked go astray; from the womb they are wayward, spreading lies."** Colossians 3:5 says, **"Put to death, therefore, whatever belongs to your earthly nature: sexual immorality, impurity, lust, evil desires and greed, which is idolatry."** Self-love gone wrong is what St. Paul warned about when he wrote, **"People will be lovers of themselves, lovers of money, boastful, proud, abusive, disobedient to their parents, ungrateful, unholy, without love, unforgiving, slanderous, without self-control, brutal, not lovers of the good, treacherous, rash, conceited, lovers of pleasure rather than lovers of God"** (2 Timothy 3:2-4).

Author Don Matzat coined the term *Christ-esteem* to express the reasons for appropriate self-love in distinction from humanistic self-esteem. Our worth has been reestablished by what Jesus did for us and what Jesus now is in us. Galatians 2:20 expresses it this way: **"I have been crucified with Christ and I no longer live, but Christ lives in me. The life I now live in the body, I live by faith in the Son of God, who loved me and gave himself for me."** Christ-esteem is the attitude that unlocks achievement and fulfillment in Christians. Giving God the glory for what we are and do avoids the egotistical pride that is a false self-love. Grace means we are loved, not because we deserve it but because God gives it. Love yourself because God does.

Think About It

What are some examples of how a false self-esteem or wrong self-love leads people to harm and wrong?

Do you really believe that God loves you? How do you know that to be true? (Read 1 John 4:9-11 for a true answer. The wrong answer will leave you with doubts.)

Who or what is the truthful mirror in which you can see yourself accurately?

"If you can think it, you can do it."

There are many books based on that pop psychology in the self-help section of bookstores. Certainly, it is good psychology to say that a positive attitude improves the odds of success. Public speakers do better imagining themselves in command before an audience. You don't want to go into a job interview convinced that you won't get the job. Visualization, seeing in your mind what you want to do before the attempt, has helped athletes. The golfer who visualizes the perfect shot and implants that image in his mind probably has a better chance of making the shot than if he merely relied on his swing coach. But there is more that is implied in statements like, "If you can think it, you can do it" or, "If you believe it, you can be it."

A decade and a half ago, Oprah Winfrey touted a book by Rhonda Byrne entitled *The Secret*. It's one book among many based on a so-called "law of attraction." There is no such *law*, of course, at least not in any scientific sense. The claim by Oprah and others is that a super-positive attitude coupled with focused visualization and "telling the universe what you want" will bring your way the very things you seek. Think of this "law" as a kind of psychic magnetism. An outlandish claim is that "your thoughts control the universe." This is mysticism dressed up in pseudoscientific garb. The universe is personified and replaces God. Human beings are told that they have the power to manipulate this deified universe. Commanding the universe substitutes for praying to God. That is a big lie. People are attracted to the rich and powerful in a world dominated by the media. If Oprah says it, thousands will believe it. But very few experience wealth and power, certainly not as a result of some cosmic attraction.

The power of positive thinking has a very religious connection in America. Norman Vincent Peale, a minister in the Reformed Church of America, popularized this blend of psychology and theology after World War II. His books and sermons taught that faith could have material, not just spiritual, benefits and that a positive mental attitude and belief in oneself are as important as belief in God. Robert Schuller was a sort of successor to Peale. His sermons from the Crystal Cathedral were telecast to a wide audience of people who wanted to believe that their lives could be better if only they believed it strongly. More recently, preachers of a "prosperity gospel" like Joel Osteen and Creflo Dollar have convinced followers that they can tap into material blessings from God with a faith resting in positive thinking. There is no doubt that health and wealth sermons have made the preachers wealthy, but there's little evidence that followers have enjoyed the same prosperity.

What's wrong with all this is that it makes promises that the Bible doesn't make and substitutes material well-being for a relationship with God based on forgiveness won by Jesus Christ. A prosperity gospel is no gospel at all. Rather than God's grace and Jesus Christ, a person's positive thinking takes center stage. The emphasis is on believing (and believing the wrong thing) and not on the God whose love inspires faith. Great spiritual harm occurs when people are directed away from Jesus to themselves and then promised what can't be delivered. If you don't get wealthy and your cancer doesn't disappear, is it because you didn't believe enough or pray enough? Or is it because God doesn't like you after all? Disillusioned followers seldom blame the preacher or recognize the deception. Spiritual and psychological damage is a too frequent result of overhyped positive thinking.

Christianity doesn't promise you a life on earth untroubled by problems and surrounded by wealth. God tells you the truth. Life in the aftermath of the fall into sin will include suffering, maybe more suffering for confessing Christ. We are called to take up our cross and follow Jesus, not look for easy roads to material prosperity. Not a better life here and now, but an eternal life of bliss and joy with Jesus, is the hope God offers. If God chooses to bless us with health and wealth, then give *him* the glory, not some law of attraction. Understand that you cannot do with positive thinking what God does not will for you. Here's what the apostle James wrote: **"Now listen, you who say, 'Today or tomorrow we will go to this or that city, spend a year there, carry on business and make money.' Why, you do not even know what will happen tomorrow. What is your life? You are a mist that appears for a little while and then vanishes. Instead, you ought to say, 'If it is the Lord's will, we will live and do this or that.' As it is, you boast in your arrogant schemes. All such boasting is evil"** (James 4:13-16).

Think About It

How can Christians understand the truth of God's law that they are sinners from birth without thereby becoming depressed about themselves and their lives?

How would you express positive thinking in a way that honors God and conforms to his truth?

What control *do* you have over your life? And what does the Bible mean by *self-control*? (Read 2 Peter 1:5–8 to get your thinking started.)

"It's okay as long as nobody gets hurt."

This rationalization has several versions. "I'm not hurting anybody" is the excuse for doing illegal drugs. "What she doesn't know won't hurt her" is a self-justification for blowing grocery money at a strip joint. "No harm, no foul" minimizes a lie that gets a person out of a tough spot at work. Maybe you've heard a version of the rationalization applied to shoplifting in this way: "Don't worry, insurance will cover it." "Consenting adults" is the argument for sex apart from marriage because nobody got hurt. Examine the rationalization and you discover that the standard for right and wrong has shifted from the act to a result. And the result is a guess or a bet, since too many consequences are unforeseen. When we get to determine what is a "hurt" and whether it will occur, we become the arbiters of right and wrong. And that job belongs to God.

> **The standard for right and wrong has shifted.**

The obvious problem with "nobody gets hurt" is that we don't know what unintended consequences may result from our actions. Does our lie to the boss result in a decision he makes that costs the company a customer? What damage to a marriage may pornography cause even though the spouse doesn't know about it? Less obvious is that we can't measure the kind of hurt or level of hurt that others may experience because of what we've said or done. Verbal abuse may masquerade as just sarcasm, but the object of repeated sarcasm may carry an invisible wound.

Every sin causes hurt to the sinner, distancing the sinner from God. Every unrepented sin chips away at the spiritual life and health of the sinner. Every sin hurts the God who calls himself our Father and seeks to draw us into a closer relationship with him. Recurring sins make us uncomfortable even thinking about God. There are, in reality, no pain-free moral wrongs. Sin hurts God, even if there were no human beings injured. Before rampant wickedness led God to send the flood, Genesis 6:6 tells us, **"The Lord regretted that he had made human beings on the earth, and his heart was deeply troubled."**

In 1 Corinthians chapter 10, the apostle Paul establishes a different set of criteria to measure if something is okay: **"No one should seek their own good, but the good of others." "Do not cause anyone to stumble** [in their faith-walk with God].**" "So whether you eat or drink or whatever you do, do it all for the glory of God"** (verses 24,32,31). In the Sermon on the Mount, Jesus set the bar for sin not only higher than whether anyone got hurt but well beyond what people do. **"You have heard that it was said, 'You shall not commit adultery.' But I tell you that anyone who looks at a woman lustfully has already committed adultery with her in his heart"** (Matthew 5:27,28).

When God brought down the walls of Jericho, he commanded Israel not to take any plunder for themselves. A man named Achan figured that grabbing some silver and gold was no big deal. Nobody got hurt. But God was hurt, and when he withdrew his power from Israel's army, 36 men died and the people's confidence in Israel's mission was damaged. Achan paid with his life for what seemed like nobody got hurt. Consequences.

King David thought his adultery with Bathsheba would hurt nobody if he could cover it up by encouraging Bathsheba's husband to sleep with her. But that failed, and David resorted to thinly veiled murder to get the husband out of the picture. He then married Bathsheba as though that would make his adultery okay. It kept getting harder to cover up the sin. God sent the prophet Nathan to confront David with the hurt his lust had caused to the moral perspective of Israel, because if the king could get away with it, then why shouldn't his subjects? And that hurt to Israel's morality necessitated the death of the baby who was the result of David's sin. Unintended consequences.

Ananias and Sapphira were a couple in the early church in Jerusalem. To support poor Christians, especially those whose livelihood had been destroyed by economic persecution, the apostles encouraged generous giving. Ananias and Sapphira sold some property in order to contribute to the cause. However, they claimed to be giving the whole amount that the sale realized when they were actually keeping some of it for themselves. It seemed just a little lie to make themselves look good; nobody got hurt. But that isn't how God saw it. **"Then Peter said, 'Ananias, how is it that Satan has so filled your heart that you have lied to the Holy Spirit and have kept for yourself some of the money you received for the land? Didn't it belong to you before it was sold? And after it was sold, wasn't the money at your disposal? What made you think of doing such a thing? You have not lied just to human beings but to God.' When Ananias heard this, he fell down and died. And great fear seized all who heard what had happened"** (Acts 5:3-5). Consequences.

The Bible gives us real-life lessons to counter the rationalization that sets aside God's commandments if nobody seems likely to get hurt. Right and wrong are established by God, commands and not suggestions, absolute and not relative to the situation, objective and not conditioned by our estimation of the outcome. Here's what God said through Moses: **"Do not add to what I command you and do not subtract from it, but keep the commands of the Lord your God that I give you"** (Deuteronomy 4:2).

Think About It

Why do we think of our wrongdoing in terms of what it may do to others rather than what it does to our relationship with God?

Think about sins against each of the Ten Commandments as to whether anyone gets hurt. How are these sins rationalized? For example, there's the term, "no fault divorce."

How does *truth* get hurt by our seemingly innocuous sins?

"It's just sex."

Casual sex is the term for it—sex that doesn't mean anything, sex without responsibility or commitment. "Friends with benefits," "one-night stands," "hookups"— our culture has created a whole vocabulary for what not long ago was more clearly identified as fornication or adultery. How did so much change so fast? Contraceptives and abortion took the fear of an unwanted child out of casual sex. Medication makes the effects of sexually transmitted diseases more tolerable. But there's more to the question of how "it's just sex" could be accepted by so many. Marriage no longer meant "till death do us part." Morality became a personal choice. Selfishness replaced caring. "Making love" degenerated into "it's just sex."

But is it "just sex"? Can telling yourself that you can separate sex from commitment make it so? Is it true that nobody got hurt? Only the calloused can separate the physical act of sexual intercourse from the emotions that surround sex. "I thought he'd call" or, "Didn't it mean anything?" express feelings that may surprise the person who thought sex was just a fling. Nobody says, "Will you still respect me in the morning?" when there was no respect to begin with. Maybe some people can view promiscuous sex without guilt, but don't be sure that their partners can. And sexual history follows a person into marriage, often disruptively.

Does anyone say, "It's just money" when she gambles away the family's life savings? Such gambling means a whole lot more than just money. Can saying, "I didn't mean anything by it" remove the hurt caused by a criticism? Can you take Christ out of Christmas? I suppose you can, but what you have left isn't really Christmas; it's just a holiday. Sex was God's gift to marriage. It consummated the "one flesh" relationship that God intended marriage to be. It was intended to express love and commitment, a shared bond that would extend to children and override disagreements about a budget. In first century Corinth, people could say, "It's just sex" because immorality knew few bounds. The apostle Paul expressed God's disagreement: **"Do you not know that he who unites himself with a prostitute is one with her in body? For it is said, 'The two will become one flesh.' Flee from sexual immorality. All other sins a person commits are outside the body, but whoever sins sexually, sins against their own body"** (1 Corinthians 6:16,18). Sex implies a one-flesh relationship.

Separating sex from marriage is fraudulent.

Separating sex from marriage is fraudulent. Here's how seriously God takes sex. The law given to Moses required marriage if there was sex. Deuteronomy 22:28,29 says, **"If a man happens to meet a virgin who is not pledged to be married and rapes her and they are discovered, he shall pay her father fifty shekels of silver. He must marry the young woman, for he has violated her. He can never divorce her as long as he lives."**

In warning about sexual temptation, Proverbs 6:27 says, **"Can a man scoop fire into his lap without his clothes being burned?"** It's an apt illustration. Fire is a good thing when it is confined to a stove or a fireplace, but fire without boundaries is destructive. Similarly, sex within marriage is a great blessing, but outside of marriage sex can be destructive. Sexual lust is like fire. St. Paul had this advice for the unmarried: **"But if they cannot control themselves, they should marry, for it is better to marry than to burn with passion"** (1 Corinthians 7:9). People may try to convince themselves that sex can be recreational—no more than an experience of short-term pleasure—but they do so in opposition to God, and that's never a good thing.

Interestingly, the Baal worship that plagued Old Testament Israel and the Greco-Roman polytheism of the first century both associated sex with worship. Temple prostitutes were a part of the fertility religion that worshiped Baal and the hedonism associated with Astarte, the goddess of fertility and sexuality. Sex as an expression of worship seems strange until you understand adultery as idolatry. St. Paul described sexual immorality as idolatry in Romans 1:24,25: **"Therefore God gave them over in the sinful desires of their hearts to sexual impurity for the degrading of their bodies with one another. They exchanged the truth about God for a lie, and worshiped and served created things rather than the Creator."** To ignore the commandments of God is to make selfish pleasure one's god. There is no such thing as "just sex."

Mercifully, the God who created sex for marriage is also the God who sent his Son to die for the sexual sins that damage marriage. The guilt that is a consequence of casual sex is washed away in the Savior's blood. Seek him; sex is no substitute.

Think About It

How is sex depicted in movies and television? What impact does that have on people's understanding of sex?

Should public schools teach about sex? How?

How does "it's just sex" exemplify the broader issue of truth? (If there is your truth and my truth rather than *the* truth, then why not my view of sex that doesn't have to be the same as your view of sex?)

"Don't be so intolerant."

That may be an appropriate challenge. We can be condescending, as though we're too smart to listen to someone else's opinion. We can marginalize people who look different or think different from us. Bigotry, racism, and sexism are intolerant positions we may adopt without even realizing it. We all tend to look at life through our own windows, shaped by our education and experience as well as the influence of others. We too easily become suspicious of people who don't share our view of things. Our polarized culture could use more tolerance. Protesters concerned for racial justice and counterprotesters upset by the destruction of property would do well to listen to each other. Tolerance could mean that we learn something from people who see issues like vaccination and masks or climate change and the national debt different from the way we see them.

Sometimes, though, the charge of intolerance is just a dodge, a way of dismissing information that people don't want to deal with. It has become a strategy for avoiding or bad-mouthing truth. For some people, being tolerant means agreeing with them, not merely listening to them. Tolerance should mean recognizing and respecting the rights and beliefs of others, not necessarily endorsing them. So if you want to defund the police and I don't, tolerance means that we don't attack each other. Tolerance means not interfering with or prohibiting what we personally don't like, as long as laws are observed. So get a permit and march in support of your convictions, but don't break the windows of my house. Have you noticed that sometimes the people who argue most vociferously for tolerance are themselves intolerant?

Everyone places limits on what we should tolerate. Who would tolerate child pornography or sex trafficking? Americans treasure freedom of speech, but hate speech is prosecutable. The problem is, who decides what is hate speech? What are the limits of tolerance when truth is at stake? For a Christian, what God commands or forbids crosses the line of tolerance. Tolerate people, yes, but not claims and arguments that contradict God's Word. You may have the right to advocate for gay marriage and multiple genders, but you don't have the right to impose your ideas on my children. There are limits on tolerance.

It is not intolerance to voice God's truth in a loving manner. In fact, it would be unfaithfulness not to do so. The charge of intolerance has become a weapon to silence Christian witness. Christians need to see through the subterfuge and kindly push back. Jude 3 says: **"I felt compelled to write and urge you to contend for the faith that was once for all entrusted to God's holy people."** Amid persecution, Christians in the first century were intimidated into silence. It is little different today. When we speak God's truth, not our own opinion, we can let others argue with God.

> **It is not intolerance to voice God's truth in a loving manner.**

Often accompanying the charge of intolerance is a statement like this: "I thought you Christians weren't supposed to judge others." It seems that people can dismiss the rest of the Sermon on the Mount while settling on Matthew 7:1: **"Do not judge, or you too will be judged."** Did Jesus mean that we should never make a moral judgment? Hardly. Read verse 1 with the subsequent verses, and it is clear that what Jesus condemned was hypocritical judging, passing judgment on the sins of others while ignoring one's own sins. Christians will avoid judging the motives of others as well as nonmoral issues such as how a person dresses or what political party he belongs to. But the Bible insists that Christians make sound judgments about truth and morality. For example, Proverbs 3:21 says, **"My son, do not let wisdom and understanding out of your sight, preserve sound judgment and discretion."** First Thessalonians 5:21,22 says this of moral arguments and truth claims: **"Test them all; hold on to what is good, reject every kind of evil."** The apostle Paul went so far as to write, **"The person with the Spirit makes judgments about all things, but such a person is not subject to merely human judgments"** (1 Corinthians 2:15).

It would be ungodly judging to point out the errors of others in order to look or feel superior to them. Scripture has a different motive. Galatians 6:1 says, **"Brothers and sisters, if someone is caught in a sin, you who live by the Spirit should restore that person gently."** Think of this as an intervention, caring and concerned friends confronting someone who is hurting herself and others by what she is doing. The motive is love. And that distinguishes what God asks of us from mere tolerance. We don't want to tolerate people. We want to love them.

Think About It

Clearly, Christians cannot be tolerant of falsehood and wickedness. But how do we help each other avoid intolerance when the issue is our political convictions?

St. Paul sets up the "love chapter," 1 Corinthians chapter 13, with the words: **"And yet I will show you the most excellent way"** (12:31). Then he continues, **"Love is patient, love is kind. It does not envy, it does not boast, it is not proud. It does not dishonor others, it is not self-seeking, it is not easily angered, it keeps no record of wrongs. Love does not delight in evil but rejoices with the truth"** (13:4-6). How do these inspired words answer people who say, "Don't be so intolerant"?

Think about things that you tolerate that your parents would not have tolerated. Which cross the line that God's Word establishes?

"YOLO"

If you aren't current on texting shorthand, YOLO stands for "You Only Live Once." At first glance that sounds almost biblical. Hebrews 9:27 says, **"People are destined to die once, and after that to face judgment."** In other words, there is no such thing as reincarnation. YOLO can also be understood to mean that we should take advantage of opportunities with calculated decisions. The Latin motto *carpe diem*, "seize the day," is similar. A senior citizen's bucket list might be a version of YOLO, an encouragement to do the things you've always wanted to. But that's not what is usually meant when someone texts YOLO.

The text message typically explains why someone made a rash decision or engaged in reckless behavior. It's an excuse for a carefree, do-what-you-feel-like approach to life that includes irresponsible risks. What has been called "stupid human tricks" would be covered by YOLO. An affluent society has meant that people don't have to worry about the basic needs of life. They have money to spend and freedom to experiment. There is little concern for the consequences of their actions or the impact of their decisions on others. In Proverbs 3:21 Solomon warns, **"My son, do not let wisdom and understanding out of your sight, preserve sound judgment and discretion."**

Maybe you can write this off as young people who think they're invincible just expressing their inexperience, but YOLO is more accurately a philosophy of life. Postmodern culture is experience focused, not reason or logic driven. Thrill seeking is the ultimate experience. Satisfying urges with instant gratification becomes a way of life. On a small scale, that might mean bungee jumping off a bridge. But it may also mean sex with a stranger or racing your car at 100 miles per hour down a city street. There is another texting acronym,

FOMO—Fear Of Missing Out—that drives bad decisions and risky behavior. The entertainment industry and social media fuel the desire to experience thrills without regrets. While living *in* the moment is a message about appreciating life as it occurs, living *for* the moment is the encouragement to indulge in whatever stimulates your senses.

Maybe you recall how the devil offered Jesus a YOLO temptation and even supported it with a Bible passage. The account is in Matthew chapter 4: **"Then the devil took him to the holy city and had him stand on the highest point of the temple. 'If you are the Son of God,' he said, 'throw yourself down. For it is written: "He will command his angels concerning you, and they will lift you up in their hands, so that you will not strike your foot against a stone"'"** (verses 5,6). Hopefully, you also remember how Jesus answered the devil: **"It is also written: 'Do not put the Lord your God to the test'"** (verse 7). YOLO too easily becomes tempting God.

YOLO too easily becomes tempting God.

St. Paul's counsel to this generation is expressed in Ephesians 5:15-17: **"Be very careful, then, how you live—not as unwise but as wise, making the most of every opportunity, because the days are evil. Therefore do not be foolish, but understand what the Lord's will is."** If we only live once, our goal should be to make our lives count. Serving others, working for justice, raising godly children, supporting causes that honor God's will—there are more than enough fulfilling objectives for life. And if you need some danger in your life, carry out these godly pursuits in a Third World country.

A British missionary named C. T. Studd, who lived a century ago, wrote a poem that says it well:

Only one life, yes only one,
Soon will its fleeting hours be done;
Then in "that day" my Lord to meet,
And stand before His Judgment seat;
Only one life, 'twill soon be past,
Only what's done for Christ will last.

In reality, we don't only live once. YOLO ignores the eternal life that Jesus won for us, the life that gives perspective to the here and now. While we live *in* the now, we do not live *for* the now. St. Paul is honest about life in this fallen world and confident about the world to come when he writes in Romans 8:18, **"I consider that our present sufferings are not worth comparing with the glory that will be revealed in us."**

Think About It

"I dare you to do it" was the challenge that kids once issued to spur risky behavior. How is YOLO an adult version of the same thing?

If YOLO expresses a felt need to give life meaning through thrilling experiences, how can we use that desire for meaning as a basis for Christian witness?

FOMO, fear of missing out, describes the sense that following Jesus may keep us from some of the pleasures that worldly people get to enjoy. What are you missing out on?

To Tell the Truth

When someone says the words "to tell you the truth," do you assume that up to this point she's been lying? Do you really expect that what she says next is the whole truth? People lie. Spouses cheat. Businesses steal intellectual property. Governments spread disinformation. It's easy to become cynical about the truth. That makes it difficult to build trusting relationships. It makes us less willing to be open with those around us. The prophet Isaiah said of the people in his day, **"We have made a lie our refuge and falsehood our hiding place"** (Isaiah 28:15). A society that doesn't value truth desensitizes us to our own lies. Christians may unwittingly make fudging the truth and hiding behind lies "normal." How serious can lying be?

The God of truth hates lying. Proverbs chapter 6 says so: **"There are six things the LORD hates, seven that are detestable to him: haughty eyes, a lying tongue, hands that shed innocent blood, a heart that devises wicked schemes, feet that are quick to rush into evil, a false witness who pours out lies and a person who stirs up conflict in the community"** (verses 16-19). Did you notice that the passage speaks of lying twice amid this litany of evil? In fact, "stirring up conflict in the community" is another description of lying and a condemnation of what is occurring in contemporary life. When lying becomes a way of life, God's truth isn't heard. When people expect a lie,

> **When lying becomes a way of life, God's truth isn't heard.**

loving relationships suffer. So central to God's will for his world is truth that in Proverbs God puts lying on the same level as murder. Killing truth is a serious sin.

Here's what St. Paul wrote to the Colossians: **"Now you must also rid yourselves of all such things as these: anger, rage, malice, slander, and filthy language from your lips. Do not lie to each other, since you have taken off your old self with its practices and have put on the new self, which is being renewed in knowledge in the image of its Creator"** (3:8-10). Telling the truth is a characteristic of the new life in Christ we are given, and truth telling is especially vital to relationships among Christians. Commit yourself to speaking the truth.

One important reason for Christians not to lie is that our mission in life is impacted by how we handle the truth. When you earn a reputation for telling the truth, you earn the right to tell THE TRUTH. People who don't know Jesus as their Savior are suspicious of the church as much as they doubt politicians and used car salesmen (sorry about that proverbial cheap shot if you sell used cars). They think churches are manipulative, seeking converts but lacking integrity. Every moral failing by a pastor and every questionable teaching by a church is magnified in the media, furthering the lack of trust people have in the church. You can disarm those suspicions with truth telling. You can be the follower of Jesus who lets people see, and then hear, the love of the Savior.

Telling others about Jesus, *the* Truth, is impeded by a culture that ridicules Christian teaching and conviction. That is not new. St. Peter introduced his encouragement to share the faith by saying, "Do not be frightened." Here are those words: **"'Do not fear their threats; do not be frightened.' But in your hearts revere Christ as Lord. Always be prepared to give an answer to everyone who asks you to give the reason for the hope that you have. But do this with gentleness and respect, keeping a clear conscience, so that**

those who speak maliciously against your good behavior in Christ may be ashamed of their slander" (1 Peter 3:14–16). Gentleness and respect are Christian characteristics that put others at ease and build conversational bridges across which truth can be shared.

In an atmosphere of lies, the truth stands out. God's truth is self-authenticating. The Holy Spirit uses truth to convict and convince people who want to know that there is something they can believe in. The truth is stronger than lies. Tell it.

Soli Deo Gloria

Dr. Paul Kelm

About the Writer

Dr. Paul Kelm is a retired pastor who served as a church planter in New England, a campus pastor, and a church consultant among other roles. He and his wife, Lynne, a retired teacher, have three children and six grandchildren.

About Time of Grace

Time of Grace is an independent, donor-funded ministry that connects people to God's grace—his love, glory, and power—so they realize the temporary things of life don't satisfy. What brings satisfaction is knowing that because Jesus lived, died, and rose for all of us, we have access to the eternal God—right now and forever.

To discover more, please visit timeofgrace.org or call 800.661.3311.

Help share God's message of grace!

Every gift you give helps Time of Grace reach people around the world with the good news of Jesus. Your generosity and prayer support take the gospel of grace to others through our ministry outreach and help them experience a satisfied life as they see God all around them.

Give today at timeofgrace.org/give or by calling 800.661.3311.

Thank you!